The Basic Essentials of
MAP AND COMPASS

D0017335

by Cliff Jacobson

**Illustrations by
Cliff Moen**

**ICS BOOKS, Inc.
Merrillville, Indiana**

THE BASIC ESSENTIALS OF MAP & COMPASS

DEDICATION

To my friend and gracious advisor, Bjorn Kjellstrom, whose love of magnetism redefined the compass.

Published by:

ICS BOOKS, Inc.
1370 E. 86th Place
Merrillville, IN 46410

CREDITS

Thanks should be extended to the following magazines:
    Canoe Magazine for allowing me to use portions of my article, *"Compasses for Canoeists,"* which appeared in the March, 1988 issue.
    Alberta Tourism and Small Business, for allowing me to reprint a portion of an Alberta road map.

Library of Congress Cataloging-in-Publication Data

Jacobson, Cliff.
  Map and compass.

  (The Basic essentials series)
  Includes index.
  1. Hiking--United States. 2. Wilderness areas--
United States. 3. Orientation--United States.
4. Maps. 5. Compass. I. Title.
GV199.4.J33 1988   796.5'1'0973   88-22965
ISBN 0-934802-42-4

TABLE OF CONTENTS

FOREWORD

A not-so-funny thing is happening to folks who use federal recreation areas: they're being told that overcrowding of certain popular routes has necessitated establishment of a *"visitor distribution"* system. Put plainly, this means that a special use permit — issued in limited numbers on a first come, first served basis — is required to hike or camp in specified portions of government managed back country.

"Visitor distribution," "special use," "travel permit" — whatever you call it, it's an essential inconvenience, one designed to minimize environmental impact on the land and to promote a high quality wilderness experience for everyone.

But not everyone agrees with the federal planners, least of all the come-latelies who are computer routed into unfavorable spots.

Roger Grosslein, environmental education specialist for the Minnesota Department of Natural Resources, summarizes: *"It's simply a matter of too many people wanting to use the same piece of ground at the same time. There are lots of wild places left for those who aren't afraid to leave the trails."*

Managers of America's most heavily used national park, the Great Smokies (which is visited by around 10 million people a year) agree. At least 50,000 people camp in the park each season, while tens of thousands hike portions of the 68 miles of Appalachian trail contained within its boundaries. Almost no one leaves the trail — which has been defiled in every way imaginable — to strike out into the remote backcountry.

Bluntly, I pressed Roger for a solution. *"Give 'em the skills to be comfortable in the wilds ... and teach 'em how to use a map and compass. They'll leave the trails only if they're sure they won't get lost."*

Admittedly, my talk with Grosslein goes back some 10 years. But nothing has changed. Overcrowding of wilderness areas still exists, and the numbers of lost hikers and hunters grow each year. Even experienced hunters and fishermen seldom know how to use a map and compass effectively. Fact is, most deer are shot within 200 yards of a road, and most fish are taken within sight of the mainland. It's a brave (or rather, *"knowledgeable"*) hunter who will venture into the deep woods, and an equally brave fisherman who will forgo the shoreline for the lure of distant islands. Only about half of all deer hunters carry a compass; almost none have maps. The record for big lake fishermen is equally dismal.

It was with these thoughts that the Minnesota Department of Natural Resources decided to develop a wilderness navigation curriculum which could be used by schools, nature centers and sportsmens' groups. The DNR agreed to furnish the technical expertise if I'd do the writing. At the outset, I proposed that the prospective materials differ from existing orienteering formats by emphasizing backcountry *navigation*, not competitive orienteering. Though navigational procedures are the same regardless of *"where"* you use your compass, orienteerers have some real advantages over those who travel the lakes and forests.

For example, the orienteering game relies on deadly accurate large scale maps, which have magnetic declination lines drawn in. Lucky is the wilderness traveler who has such a *"thoughtful"* picture to guide the way. More often than not, outdoors people must make do with outdated topographic maps or state park guides. Sure ... good maps are available for just about every place in north America, but for one reason or other, most folks don't have them. Wilderness navigation then, should include the *"way things are"* as well as *"how they ought to be."*

As I worked on the project, I discovered that outdoor enthusiasts would rather *"do"* than read; that probing complex route-finding procedures served only to confuse, while over-simplifying processes gave false confidence. And that the interpretation of contour lines — an essential component of land navigation — could, after the presentation of a few simple rules, be mastered by beginners in a matter of minutes.

So along with the help of DNR experts, I wrote, revised, wrote again. Ultimately, we developed a simplified approach to route finding, the rudiments of which I've incorporated here. If you proceed step-by-step through the chapters you'll have no trouble navigating the backcountry. That's a promise!

EQUIPMENT YOU NEED

It's pointless to begin the study of wilderness route-finding without the two most important tools — a map and compass. So before you begin your study, please assemble the following materials:

1. An *"Orienteering"* style compass. No other type works as well. Indeed, you will be severely handicapped by any other instrument. You'll find a thorough discussion of *all types* of compasses in chapter 3, and Appendix 1 provides specific model recommendations. Excellent Orienteering compasses can be purchased for under 10 dollars.

2. Space and cost considerations prevent us from including a colored topographic *"practice"* map. Instead, we've downsized selected portions of full size maps, pinpointing the information you need to know. While this should pose no learning difficulty, you may get the *"big picture"* more quickly if you have on hand a genuine topographic map which contains all the *"pieces of the puzzle"* on a single page.

Any topo map will do, though, the larger the scale, the better. A 1:24,000 (about 2.5 inches to the mile) American map, or a 1:50,000 (1.25 inches equals one mile) Canadian map is ideal. Why not get a map of your favorite hunting, fishing or hiking area? Chapter 1 tells you how to order maps.

3. An inexpensive plastic protractor is a *must* if you don't have an Orienteering style compass. Otherwise, it's surplus baggage.

1. MAPS — GETTING STARTED

Some years ago, while on a canoe trip in the Boundary Waters Canoe Area of Minnesota, I rounded a point and saw a young couple sitting dolefully on a rock, staring intently at what appeared to be a map. When they saw me, the pair stood up and waved frantically in my direction. Curiously, I paddled over, only to discover the two were hopelessly lost.

The man told me they'd left the lodge the day before and had set out with a complement of backpacking gear to hike a portion of the Kekakabic trail — an old fire road which runs from Ely to Grand Marais. The trail crosses a number of area lakes, hence our chance meeting. But the trail is poorly marked and it's not maintained. Numerous animal trails and canoe portages intersect the route and confuse things considerably. A good compass and topo map are essential tools for navigating the Kek.

The man poured coffee while the woman continued to study the map. *"I think we're here,"* she said, tapping her finger on what appeared to be a small knoll near the water's edge. Eagerly, she looked to me for reinforcement.

I squinted wonderingly at the impossibly small scale (1:500,000) map. Even with my bifocals, I could tell nothing.

"Where'd you get this map?" I questioned. *"From our outfitter,"* came the reply.

"Hmmm ..." I walked back to the canoe and got my 1:50,000 topo map and spread it out on the lichen-splashed outcrop.

"I believe you're here," I said, pointing to a drumlin some distance from the perceived location. *"How can you guys find your way around up here with a map like this?"*

"We can't!" came the ready answer. *"Our outfitter said this was all we needed, that it'd work fine."*

"Yeah," I replied.

Fortunately, I had three sets of maps in my party, so parting with one caused no inconvenience.

As the case illustrates, you can't do good work without the right tools. A good map is *"everything."* A compass alone won't do. A compass is useful *only* if you know what to set on it. And for that you need a map.

Figure 1-1

Even a simple state park or road map is better than no map at all. Example: Assume you're lost in the heavily wooded area in figure 1-1; You have a compass but no map. And no idea where you parked your car or *"went in."* Being lost comes as quite a surprise. After all, you hadn't planned on going in *"that far."*

Realistic problem? You bet! Ask any excited deer hunter. Think hard. How can you find your way out of the woods?

There is one way. It's called luck. Maybe if you go in a straight line (on any compass bearing) far enough, you'll hit a road. Maybe …!

Now, let's re-do the problem with the aid of a highway map (Figure 1-2). Only this time we can be more specific. You're cruising southeast on highway 2, along the edge of Glacier National Park. You park somewhere along the roadway then strike off roughly northeast into the bush. You stuff map and compass deep into your pockets. Surely you won't need them. After all, you're going only *"a short distance."*

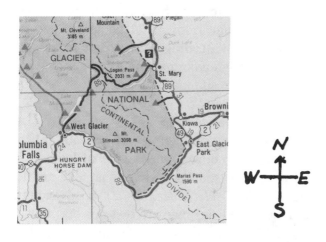

Figure 1-2   Road map of Glacier National Park

Several hours later, your enthusiasm dampens. Edged against a stand of impenetrable pines, miles of *"nothing"* stand between you and your car. Now what?

Easy, Your highway map shows that roads border the woods all around. Granted, there's not much detail, but it's enough. A rough south-southwest bearing will bring you back to highway 2. From then on, it's simply a matter of asking directions.

As you can see, even a gas station highway map or state park guide will *"get you out of the woods,"* if you have a compass and can use it for finding rough directions.

Beyond Planimetric Maps

Trouble with road maps and state park guides is that they're *"planimetric,"* which means they show topography in a dead flat perspective. Hills and valleys don't mean much when you're driving a car. But put on your hiking boots and the mood changes. For cross country — indeed *any* — wilderness travel, you need a map which shows all the ups and downs, plus major stoppers like swamps and canyon walls. *"Topographic"* maps, as they are called, provide a three dimensional perspective of the land.

Topographic Map Scales

All modern maps are made from aerial photographs which give a precise picture of the land. Cartographers (map makers) use these photos to construct topographic maps in a variety of scales, the most common of which are summarized below:

For American Maps

1:250,000 (1/250,000): One unit on the map equals 250,000 units on the ground. Each map covers one degree of latitude and two degrees of longitude (see discussion of latitude and longitude in the next section.) We Americans still work and think in the English system and our maps reflect our bias towards *"inches"* and *"feet."* Here, one inch on the map equals 250,000 inches, or almost exactly *four* miles on the ground. As you might guess, one to a quarter million maps don't show much detail.

1:62,500: Also called *"15 minute series,"* each map covers 15 minutes of latitude and 15 minutes of longitude. There are 63,360 inches to the mile, close enough so that these maps provide a working relationship of 1 inch = 1 mile. This is probably the most useful and practical scale for backcountry use.

1:24,000 (7.5 minute series): One inch on the map equals 2,000 feet on the ground. Works out to a bit more than 2-1/2 inches to the mile. These large scale maps are great for precision navigation but each one covers only about 55 square miles of territory, which means you'll need a lot of them if you're traveling very far. And at around three bucks per sheet, costs mount quickly.

For Canadian Maps

1:250,000: (Same as American maps) and *1:50,000* are the most popular *traveling* maps in Canada. The 1:50's are particularly nice: Here, 1-1/4 inches equal one mile.

Colored or Monochrome?

Canadian maps in 1:50,000 scale are often available in *"monochrome"* (black and white) as well as colored editions. Consequently forests (commonly shown as *green* areas) and lakes (blue colored) will appear in varying shades of gray.

Why get monochrome maps if colored ones are available? Two reasons: they cost less and photocopy better — important considerations if you need a lot of maps or duplications of certain sheets.

Unfortunately, American maps are not available in monochrome editions.

Land Use Information Series Maps

These are standard 1:250,000 *Canadian* topo maps that are overprinted with information about wildlife, vegetation, hunting and fishing, climate and points of interest. They'll tell you where Peregrine falcons nest, the migration routes and movements of caribou, the location of various fish species and more. Land Use maps tend to be pretty cluttered with data so they're only marginally useful for navigation.

These maps are not available for all of Canada. Ask for the special *"Index to Land Use Information Series"* Maps, when you write the Canada Map Office.

Land Use and Land Cover Maps

These *American* maps are similar to Canadian Land Use Information maps, with these exceptions: *Land Use* refers to how man's activities affect the land (for example, housing and industry).

Land Cover describes the vegetation, water and artificial constructions on the land surface. Scale is 1:100,000 or 1:250,000.

Order these maps from the N.C.I.C. office nearest you.

Where To Order Maps
Order American topographic maps from:
    Branch of Distribution
    U.S. Geological Survey
    Box 25286, Federal Center
    Denver, Colorado 80225

For Alaska maps, write:
    Alaska Distribution Section
    U.S. Geological Survey
    New Federal Building, Box 12
    101 Twelfth Ave.
    Fairbanks, Alaska 99701

For charts and tide tables of U.S. coasts, the great lakes and sections of major rivers, write:
    National Ocean Survey
    Division C44
    6501 Lafayette Ave.
    Riverdale, MD 20840

The National Cartographic Information Center (N.C.I.C.) will help you find special purpose maps of all kinds. It sorts and collects cartographic information from Federal, State and local government agencies. Write the N.C.I.C. office nearest you for a listing of city, county and wilderness area (U.S. national parks and forests) maps and aerial photos. You can also get hydrographic maps for fishing, space photos, and more. N.C.I.C. will answer all your map questions ... and sell you what you need. They have a ton (well, at least five pounds) of free pamphlets.

    N.C.I.C. Headquarters
    National Cartographic Information Center
    U.S. Geological Survey
    507 National Center
    Reston, VA 22092

Western Mapping Center, N.C.I.C.
U.S. Geological Survey
345 Middlefield Rd.
Menlo Park, CA 94025

Rocky Mountain Mapping Center, N.C.I.C.
U.S. Geological Survey, Box 25046
Denver, Federal Center, Mail Stop 504
Denver, CO 80225

Midcontinent Mapping Center, N.C.I.C.
U.S. Geological Survey
1400 Independence Rd.
Rolla, MO 65401

Order Canadian topographic maps, Land Use Information Series maps and aerial photos from:

Canada Map Office
Dept. of Energy, Mines and Resources
615 Booth St.
Ottawa, Ontario KIA 0E9

For Canadian charts and tide tables:
Hydrographic Chart Distribution Office
Dept. of Fisheries and Oceans
1675 Russel Rd., P.O. Box 8080
Ottawa, Ontario K1G 3H6

You can't order maps until you know what's in print. For this, you'll need an *Index To Topographic Maps,*" available *free* from the agencies above. Several indexes cover the United States and Canada. To get the right one, simply identify the state or province of your interest.

When your index arrives (it generally takes about four weeks), you're ready to order maps. Follow the detailed ordering instructions which come with each index, and you'll have no trouble finding the map you need in the scale you want.

With your topo map in hand, you're ready to plan your route into the backcountry. Let's begin by identifying the important map features:

Map Name: You'll find the map name in the upper and lower margins of American maps, and in the lower margin of Canadian maps. American maps also have names in parentheses which indicate adjacent quadrangles. For example, the map just east of ESKO, MINN-WIS. (Figure 1-3) is WEST DULUTH.

Figure 1-3   1:24,000 map showing map names and adjacent quads.
                   (ESKO)

The Canadians use a slightly different system (Figure 1-4.) Here, the NAKINA name and location designation (42L) is included in a block diagram in the legend — a procedure which allows you to see adjacent map sheets at a glance.

Scale: You'll find the representative fraction (1:24,000, etc.) and bar scale in the lower map margin.

Date: Most topo maps are very old; some were last field-checked in the 1950's. A lot has changed since then, especially the location of roads, dams and other man-made features. The key words *"revised"* and *"field- checked,"* will tell you when these maps were last up-dated.

Certainly, an old topo map is better than none at all. But it won't do if you're a planning a *"remote"* hunting or fishing trip.

Figure 1-4   Index to adjoining sheets of National Topograhic System.
Canada map, showing "Nakina" location.

If you need more current information than that supplied by your map, contact the government agency (U.S. Forest Service, Department of Natural Resources, etc.) nearest your area of concern. These professionals require current maps for their daily work. If they can't tell you where to get the maps you need, they'll help you update yours.

Latitude and longitude: Your map is a bird's eye view of a tiny portion of the earth's surface. But where does it fit onto the *"big sphere?"* By using *latitude* and *longitude* we can reference any location to a precise spot on the globe.

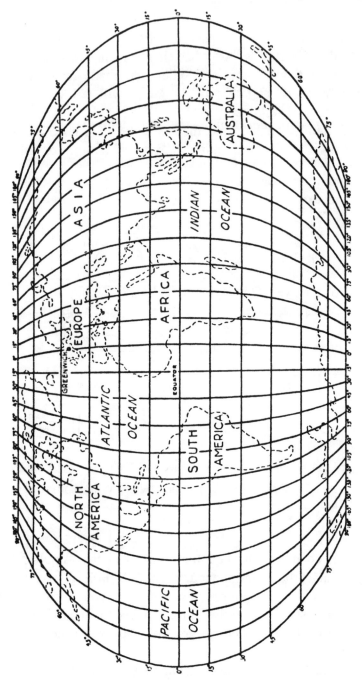

Figure 1-5   Lines of latitude run parallel to the equator. Lines of longitude
run north-south and intersect at the poles.

Lines of *latitude* (or *parallels,*) run parallel to the equator, which is zero degrees. The *"longitudinal"* north/south lines which intersect at the poles are called *"meridians"* or lines of *longitude* (Figure 1-5.) Longitude is measured in degrees east or west of the zero degree *"prime meridian,"* which originates in Greenwich, England.

By splitting latitude and longitude degree readings into smaller units, called *"minutes"* and *"seconds,"* specific points on the earth may be accurately located via a coordinate system. The rules are simple:

1° (1 degree) = 60' (minutes)

1' = 60" (seconds)

For example, *"Selkirk"* (see figure 1-6) is located at approximately 96° 55' west longitude/50° 10' north latitude.

All this is needlessly academic unless you plan to order specific large scale maps and *aerial photographs*.

Figure 1-6   Latitude/longitude of "Selkirk," Manitoba.

Aerial Photos
Suppose you're planning to canoe a remote river in Canada. Your topo says you'll have to portage your gear around a major falls along the route. However, the map does not tell you where

the portage begins. In fact, the *"contour lines"* (more on this, later) suggest there's an impassable canyon wall on both sides of the river.

Want to know more? Then order the aerial photographs from which your map was made. Photos will bring into clear perspective the most obscure features; more so, if you specify *"stereo pairs."* All you need is an inexpensive stereoscope (available at most hobby shops) to view the land in glorious 3-D. Now, you'll find a route around the falls ... if one exists!

Note: Aerial photos are expensive, and they are very large scale (somewhere between 1:24,000 and 1:60,000.) Since there are *millions* of them on file, getting exactly what you want requires *precise* identification of the specific land feature to the nearest five minutes of arc.

There is, however, a chicken route for those who don't understand the ways of latitude and longitude: Just outline your area of interest on a topo map and send it along with your check to the N.C.I.C. or Canada map office. Your map will be returned with your order.

Which Way is North?

"North," as everyone who has headed *"up"* north knows, is always at the top of the map. Well, sort of. And for conventional route finding in the American midwest, you can get by with that knowledge alone. However, if you plan to travel in the east or west, you'll need to take into account the differences between the *three* norths.

Most important, is *true*, or geographic north. That's the direction the lines of longitude run. Since the vertical lines which describe the right and left map margins are true meridians, any line on your map drawn parallel to them, runs *true* north and south. Almost!

Meridians, you see, converge towards the poles so the ones which run along your map edges *are not* truly parallel to one another (and the closer you get to each pole, the *less* parallel they become). No problem; that's what the *"neat"* lines are for.

"Neat" lines appear as tiny tick marks at equidistant points along all four map margins. To locate a true north-south meridian, simply connect the neat lines of equal value at the top and bottom

of the map (Figure 1-7 shows the relationship.) Similarly, you can plot a true east-west line (parallel) by connecting the latitude neat lines. Then, you can use these coordinates to accurately plot the latitude/longitude of any point on your map.

Figure 1-7   Locating true north/south meridian.

The Other Norths

Grid north: Topographic maps all have *"grid lines"* imprinted on their face. Grid lines began life as true meridians and parallels but became distorted when the spherical earth was flattened onto paper. Cartographers use a number of map *"projections"* to minimize this distortion, but all are subject to some small error. Consequently, grid lines usually *do not* point true north/south or true east/west.

The error is reported in a *"declination"* diagram (refer to Figure 4-8) in the bottom map margin, and is usually small enough that it can be ignored by everyone but surveyors.

"Grid north" is the north you'll want to use when working with civilian and military topographic maps. Use *true* north with maps that don't have grid lines imprinted on their face.

Magnetic north: Most everyone knows that the compass needle does not point to *true* north. Rather, it *"points"* toward the north magnetic pole which is located several hundred miles south of *"the real thing."* The angular difference between the *"three norths"* is reported in declination diagrams or legend information on all topographic maps. In chapter four we'll have a lively discussion of how this affects navigation.

Contour Lines

The thin brown lines on topographic maps are called *"contour lines."* They give *"depth"* and elevation to the land. You'll learn all about them in the next chapter.

Map Symbols

How do you tell (on a map) a school from a church? By the appropriate *"symbol,"* of course. There are dozens of map symbols, most of which are obvious. But lest you forget, Canadian maps emblazon them all in the margin or on the back. American U.S.G.S. maps are more subtle. They tease you with a few road classifications then *"assume"* you know the rest, or have on hand their free pamphlet *"Topographic Map Symbols,"* which lists them all.

How Brazen!

You'll find a listing of the most common symbols in appendix 2.

Tip: If you have an old map, don't take the location of trails, unimproved roads, churches and schools too seriously. It's quite possible that some of these *"man-made features"* no longer exist!

You should also realize that for clarity, map symbols *are not* drawn to scale — they always appear much larger than they really are. However, the *geometric center* of these symbols is accurately plotted. So shoot compass bearings (or measure) there if you need to target a particular point.

2. EASY MAP READING

Figure 2-1

Understanding Map Contours

The light brown lines overprinted on topographic maps are called *contour lines*. They indicate the elevation above sea level (sometimes, other references are used) of land features and thus permit you to view the topography in three dimensions instead of two. Entire books have been written about contour lines and their interpretation. However, you'll get along quite nicely if you master these basics:

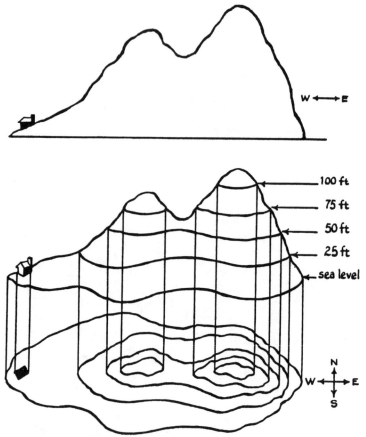

Figure 2-2   Contour lines: Mountain Island

1.   Contour lines connect points of *equal* elevation. Thus, closely spaced lines indicate lots of elevation change, whereas wide-spaced lines show the opposite (Figures 2-2). You gain or lose elevation only when you travel from one contour line to another. If you walk along a contour line, you'll be *"on the level."*

2.   The *contour interval* is the vertical distance between contour lines. Its value in feet or meters is given in the lower map margin. Thus, if the *"CI"* is 50 feet, each successive contour line on the map increases or decreases as the case may be) in elevation by exactly 50 feet. Each *fifth "Index"* contour is dark colored and is labeled with a number which gives its actual elevation above sea level.

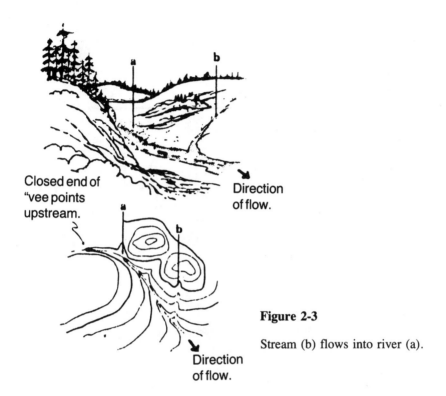

Closed end of "vee points upstream.

Direction of flow.

Direction of flow.

Figure 2-3

Stream (b) flows into river (a).

3. The contour interval is determined by the cartographer, based on the amount of elevation change in the area. Heavily mountained regions will have contour intervals of 50 feet or more, while on relative flatlands it may be ten feet or less. Consequently, the contour interval *is not* the same for all maps.

Tip: Convert meters (foreign maps are all metric to feet (1 meter equals 3.3 feet) if you don't think in the metric system.

4. The larger the contour interval, the less clear are the characteristics of the area. In short, a map whose *"CI"*is 10 feet, gives a clearer picture of the topography than one whose *"CI"* is 100 feet. Keep this fact uppermost in your mind when you plan a cross-country hiking or ski trip. Remember, the shortest distance between two points is a straight line only if you're not mountain climbing!

Figure 2-4
Falls are easy to spot on the contour map. Closely spaced "vee" points indicate a sudden drop. Notice the difference between the extreme elevation change at 300' - 250' and the long decline between 250' - 200'.

5. Where contour lines cross or run very close together, you'll find an abrupt drop — a falls or canyon (Figure 2-4.) Especially look for these closely spaced contour lines if you're boating an unknown river. If *"tight"* contours *intersect* your route. you can bet there are substantial rapids there.

To allay your concern, you may want to plot a river *"profile"* which shows the actual drop per mile.

Making the Profile

Begin by drawing a broad line along each side of the river, parallel to your route. These lines reference your route — and draw your eyes to the river — so you can quickly locate what lies ahead, without visual interference from other map features. I use a translucent felt tip *"Highliter"* pen, the kind college kids prefer for marking important passages in text books.

Next, consult the map scale and mark the miles along your route. Gear the number of markers to the map scale. For example, on 1:250,000 maps, I label every four miles (Figure 2-5,) which works out to a mark every inch. On larger scale maps I tick off each mile. The idea is to clarify without cluttering.

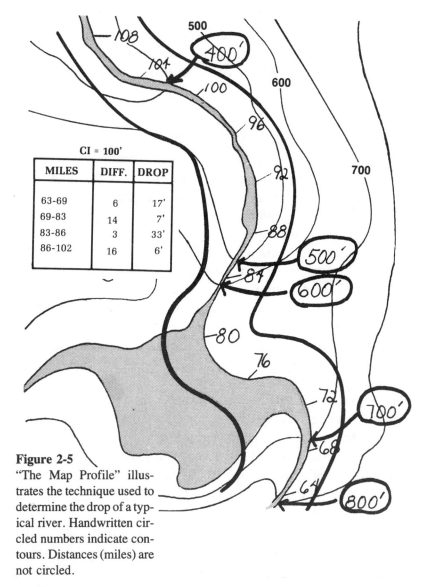

Figure 2-5
"The Map Profile" illustrates the technique used to determine the drop of a typical river. Handwritten circled numbers indicate contours. Distances (miles) are not circled.

MILES	DIFF.	DROP
63-69	6	17'
69-83	14	7'
83-86	3	33'
86-102	16	6'

CI = 100'

Now, get out your pencil and draw a small arrow everywhere a contour line crosses the river. Write in the elevations of each contour near the penciled arrow and circle it. Be sure you indicate whether the elevation is in feet or meters.

You're now ready to compute *"drop."* Do the computations in a table similar to that in Figure 2-5. For example, the 800 foot contour crosses the river at mile 63, while the 700 foot line intersects at mile 69. This is recorded in the table as *"63-69."* The mileage difference is six (63-69.) Dividing six into 100 (the value of the contour interval) yields a drop of 17 feet per mile.

From mile 69 to 83 the river drops less — seven feet per mile, etc.

In deciding if it's safe to boat an unknown river, keep these rules-of-thumb in mind:

a.   A drop of three to five feet per mile is nice cruising for an open canoe or fishing boat. Ten feet per mile means gentle rapids. Twenty or more is about the limit of an open canoe, and 35 may mean you'll have to portage your rubber raft. *Caution*: these are only guidelines! Maps tell you what to expect ... not *"what is!"* Use your *eyes* to account for that!

b.   Equally important as *"drop per mile"* is how the drops occur — whether uniformly, or at a falls, dam or major rapid. Closely spaced drops mean a probable portage at those spots, though the rest of the river may be *"user friendly."* Uniform drops suggest a wild fast ride, and your skills had best be up to it!

Note: you can convert the *"top view"* of your profile to a side view for greater clarity. Figure 2-4 shows the procedure. You can also use this same method to draw a profile for land masses. Suppose you want to hike cross-country but a large hill stands in the way. Can you walk the hill or will you have to claw up it? To find out the answer, simply draw a line from your location to your destination, and graph the drop as shown in Figure 2-4.

6.   The closed or *"vee"* end of a contour line always points upstream (Figure 2-3, 2-4). Note that this rule also applies to creeks, intermittent streams and gullies.

7.   Contour lines become *"U-shaped,"* (the closed ends of the U's point *down hill)* to indicate the outjutting spur (ridge) of a hill.

8.   The actual heights of many objects are given on topographic maps. For example, suppose you find the number 636X printed at a road junction. This means that the X-marked spot is exactly 636 feet above sea level.

CONTOUR INTERVAL 50 FEET
Elevations in Feet Above Mean Sea Level
North American Datum 1927
Transverse Mercator Projection

Figure 2-6   Contour Quiz Illustration

Contour Quiz

Use Figure 2-6 to test your knowledge of contour lines. Answers are on the next page.

1.   Is the creek flowing *into* or *out of* Pikitigushi Lake?

2.   You are standing at point (a). What is your height above sea level? (Clue: notice the 1,000 foot contour to the east.)

3.   You are standing at point (b), looking towards Pikitigushi Lake. Describe the topography directly in front of you.

4.   You are walking south, from (b) to (c). Are you a) gaining elevation? b) losing elevation? c) remaining level?

5.   You walk from (b) to (d). You are: a) going up a steep hill, b) going down a gully, c) going up a gully.

6.   A creek joins lake (e) from the west. Does that creek flow *into,* or *out of* lake (e)?

Answers To Contour Quiz

1.   Into the lake. Remember, the closed ends of a contour line point *upstream*.

2.   1250 feet. The index contour to the east is labeled 1000. The contour interval is 50 feet. 50 feet X 5 lines = 250 feet of rise.

3.   Very steep drop, almost a cliff. You wouldn't want to climb it.

4.   You lose 50 feet of elevation (you go down 100 feet to the plateau, then climb 50 feet to reach (c).

5.   (b)Down a gully.

6.   The creek flows *to the west*, out of lake *"e."*

Figure 2-7
Mark the location of (a) and (b) on your paper, then compare it to the map bar scale.

SCALE 1:24 000

Using The Bar Scale To Measure Horizontal Distances

Most of the time, maintaining map/ground scale relationships is simply a matter of remembering how many inches per mile the scale portrays, and interpolating accordingly. However, sometimes you want a more precise answer than your guestimate provides. One way is to use the *bar scale* in the map legend, and a piece of scratch paper.

To compute the distance from (a) to (b) in Figure 2-7, place the paper edge between the points and transfer this distance to the scale below. You'll get a bit less than three-fourths of a mile.

You can also measure the distance directly with the graduated base-plate of your Orienteering compass.

Preparing Your Maps For Use In The Backcountry

Maps are a joy to use if they're well organized and protected from the weather. Here are the recommended procedures:

1. Begin by outlining your route with a felt-tip *"Highlighter."* This way, you can see where you're going at a glance.

2. If you're hiking or boating on a river or lake, you'll want to *"tick off"* the miles, as explained on page 18, *"Making the Profile."* This will keep you from biting off more than you can swallow when you do your winter planning. Canoeists, kayakers and rafters should carefully designate the location of stoppers like falls and dangerous rapids, and the positioning of portage trails. To allay your concern you may want to draw a river (or trail) profile which shows actual drop per mile.

3. Maps that will be frequently used in fishing boats are best glued to a thin plywood board, then clear lacquered to protect them from water. Drill a hole in one corner of the board and attach a nylon security cord. You may also want to tie your compass to the board. Now, everything is at hand and protected from the elements.

Here are some other ways to waterproof your maps:

1. Insert them in Zip-lock plastic bags. Giant 12-1/2" X 16" Zip-locks are available from office supply stores. Camping equipment shops (and most Boy Scout supply centers) carry heavier, similar sized plastic envelopes with genuine zippers. If you want an inexpensive giant sized map case, check out your local bait shop. Four-mil thick *"minnow"* bags measure 32 X 17-1/2 inches (these are also great for sleeping bags and clothing.) Seal the mouth of these bags with duct tape.

2. Cover maps with clear contact paper — makes them waterproof, but you can't write on them.

3. Paint on *"Stormproof"* — a clear chemical that's especially formulated for use on maps and charts. Order by mail from the Martensen Company, P.O. Box 261, Williamsburg, VA 23185.

4.   Apply *"Thompson's Water Seal"* — an industrial strength chemical that's used for sealing concrete block. *"TWS"* is available in hardware stores in aerosol cans and tins. Apply it with a foam varnish brush. *"TWS"* (and *"Stormproof)"* makes maps water-repellent, not waterproof. You can write over it with pen or pencil.

5.   No sense carrying map portions that you won't use. So trim away unnecessary paper with a scissors before you leave home. If you have a number of map sheets, use either of these methods for organizing them:

a.   Glue the quadrangles together with *rubber cement,* accurately matching the latitude/longitude neat lines. Cut out important legend information and glue it to the map back or over a non-essential area.

b. Number individual map sheets consecutively. This works fine, except when you find yourself at the edge of a map sheet.

Maps which will be used in the field are better folded than rolled.

Tip: Discover *"Forestry Suppliers, Inc.,"* 205 West Rankin St., Box 8397, Jackson, Mississippi 39204. This company carries a complete line of tools for the professional forester and geologist, including dozens of map aids and laminating films for maps and journals. They carry the complete line of Silva, Suunto and Brunton compasses. Write for their catalog.

3. ANATOMY OF THE COMPASS

History

No one is certain where or how the compass originated, though it appears that the Chinese were first to discover magnetism in lodestone and its attractive power. One of the first working models consisted of a piece of lodestone floating on a cork in a bowl of water. Other primitive compasses, with magnets shaped like fish or turtles, can be seen in Chinese books which date to the 11th and 12th centuries.

The first clear description of a magnetic needle compass is by Shen Kua, a Chinese, in 1088 A.D. — about a century before the earliest mention in European texts. From then on, there are numerous references to compasses in Chinese literature, as well as stories about their use by sailors *"In dark weather or when the sky is overcast."* Other references suggest that primitive compasses were used by Arabian merchants in 1200 A.D. and by Vikings a half century later.

It is not clear whether magnetism and its use for navigation was discovered independently in Europe or brought by travelers from China.

For awhile, the Chinese led the world in compass production, evidently because the hardened steel needed to hold the magnetism was not available in other parts of the world. But around 1400-1500, Europeans got into the act and marine compasses became widely available. However, it wasn't until someone realized that compasses could be modified as sun dials — and thereby substitute for the expensive watches of the day — that portable field compasses were born.

Little change took place until the end of the pocket sun dial period, around 1750. Then came the development of sighting devices and the refinement of the *"watch"* or *"box"* compass, which survives today with few modifications.

In the 20th century, we saw substantial improvements in field compasses in the form of the Bezard compass of 1902 and the liquid-filled British army compass of world war I. But it was not until the 1930's that the real excitement began. First, came the development of reasonably priced liquid-filled Orienteering compasses and birth of the Silva company, then the introduction of protractor-combined plate compasses and sophisticated sighting devices. Things continue on the upswing: The best of today's compasses are a tribute to engineering genius — a quiet lesson in sophisticated simplicity.*

Compasses For The Nineties And Beyond

A half century ago, route-finding was a precarious business. Maps of wilderness areas were not always accurate and compasses were heavy, slow to use, not waterproof, and had no provision for computing bearings from a map.

Now, all that has changed. The best modern compasses incorporate complete navigational systems. No longer do you have to grope for a pencil and protractor, and *orient the map to north"* to take a bearing. And don't let the plastic toy-like construction of these instruments fool you. Most of the mid-priced ($10-$20) models can be *consistently* read to within two degrees of an optical transit ... hand held! Even the cheapies seldom vary by more than four degrees.

There are four types of compasses: 1)*Fixed dial* or standard

---

*I am indebted to Bjorn Kjellstrom, inventor of the Silva compass for this historic information.

needle compass; 2)*floating dial*; 3)*Cruiser*; 4)*Orienteering*. For hiking, canoeing, hunting and fishing ... and just about everything else, only the Orienteering type (and where extreme accuracy is required — the floating dial with optical sights) makes much sense. Here are the differences:

Figure 3-1

Floating dial lensatic compass.

look through here

Floating Dial Compass

The needle is an integral part of the numbered dial which spins freely on the pivot. You point the compass towards your objective and read the bearing at an index. There's nothing to set, usually, not even a cover to raise. Floating dial compasses run the gauntlet of quality — from five dollar *"hunter pin-on's"* to sophisticated direct sighting models like the Suunto KB-14 (Figure 3-1), which can be interpolated to more than 15 minutes of arc.

Figure 3-2

Fixed dial compass

Fixed Dial Compass

Best typified by 25 cent gum ball machine models, these *"questionably superior"* versions of the old *"box"* compass have degree readings embossed on a fixed outer ring (Figure 3-2.) The needle rides on a hardened steel or mineral bearing in the center of the capsule. Fixed dial compasses are slow to use, inaccurate and not very versatile. People buy them because they don't know how to use any other kind. About all these are good for is zipper pulls on jackets. Nonetheless, because they are so popular, you should know how to use them *effectively*. You'll find the specifics on page 35.

Cruiser Compasses

These are professional grade instruments which come in solid metal cases with protective hinged covers, onto which a *"lubber's"* (sighting) line has been inscribed. Numbers on the dial run counterclockwise (opposite to that of a fixed-dial compass) so you can face your objective and read the instrument where the north end of the magnetic needle intersects the dial.

Despite their dated design, *"cruisers"* are still widely used by foresters and geologists. They are accurate, heavy, slow to use, not waterproof, and very expensive.

Figure 3-3   "Orienteering" compass

Orienteering Compasses —
The Choice Of Serious Outdoorspeople

Accuracy is only half the game. The other part is determining what numerical value to set on the compass. For this, you need a map and protractor.

Enter the *Orienteering* compass. In 1933, Gunnar Tillander, an unemployed instrument worker, approached Bjorn Kjellstrom and his brothers Alvar and Arvid with a unique plan: Why not incorporate a protractor into the design of a standard needle compass? Almost overnight, the Orienteering compass was born. It is unique for these reasons:

1. You can determine bearings from a map *without* the aid of a protractor, *and* without orienting the map to north. This means you can make the computation from the seat of bobbing canoe or while shuffling down a wilderness trail. You can even do it with mittens on!

2. Your direction-of-travel (bearing) is *"locked"* onto the compass dial. There's nothing to remember or write down. In fact, you don't even have to read the dial at all!

3. All Orienteering compasses have ruled scales along their plastic base plates which make it easy to determine scale distances from a map.

4. Orienteering compasses all have liquid-damped needles. Needle oscillation ceases in three to five seconds. The system works to 40 below zero!

5. The instrument is so simple, an eight year old can learn to run one in a matter of minutes.

For backcountry use, the Orienteering compass has no peer. Unless you're running survey lines in search of buried treasure — in which case, you'll want an optical sighting compass — I can think of no reason why you should choose any other kind!

Because the Orienteering compass is so versatile, the instruction in this book is centered around its use.

Accuracy: How Much Do You Need?

Surveyors and foresters need compasses which give readings to a fraction of a degree. But for general outdoor use, any instrument which will consistently read within *four* degrees of a transit will do, even for serious expeditions. You don't need 30 minute accuracy for navigating the backcountry. What you do need is a good map and *versatile* compass.

Consider this: One degree of compass error equals 92 feet per mile (tan. 1°x 5280) of ground error. A four degree error over a mile course will cause you to miss your objective by 368 feet — hardly significant when you consider *how* compasses are actually used. For example, rather than risk missing their objective (even by 368 feet), experienced travelers *"aim-off."* That is, they make a purposeful error to the left or right of their reference point. Then, they follow a road, trail, shoreline, powerline, or other *"hand-rail"* to their destination. Figure 4-5 in the next chapter details the procedure.

"Aiming-off" becomes even more important when you realize that man-made features, like buildings and trails, are frequently

mis-plotted on maps. Under these conditions, clear thinking is more important than precise headings. Here's what you need most in a *"working"* compass:

1. *Versatility* in transferring bearings from map to ground — hence, the desirability of the Orienteering compass.

2. *Speed of operation:* Often, you need to determine a direction from the seat of a bobbing canoe or fishing boat.

3. *Carryability:* Consider your compass an article of clothing, one you'll wear all the time. The lighter and more compact the instrument, the more pleasurable it will be to carry. Particularly, shun any compass with sharp, square edges. *"Square corners"* may be great for map plotting, but they'll eat through your clothes in a matter of minutes.

4. *Durability*: I once had a jeep run over an old Silva Ranger. The cover was smashed but the instrument worked fine. That's tough! A field compass must be built to take everything from a bad fall to a thorough dousing.

5. *Amenities*: Are the scales on the base plate compatible with those on your map? Can the compass be compensated for area magnetic declination? (see Chapter 4 for details). Night sights — either luminous or (better) a lithium light is essential for black night travel. And if you're over 40, a built-in magnifying glass will clarify map subtleties.

Damping

A compass needle will continue to oscillate for some time unless it is *"damped,"* either by a light viscosity liquid (liquid damping) or by magnetism (induction damping.) Liquid-damped needles stop moving in about three seconds; induction damped needles take much longer. As to longevity, the vote goes to induction damping, as there's never a chance for a leaky capsule. However, induction damped instruments are usually heavier, bulkier and more expensive than liquid damped ones. Nearly all the best hand compasses are currently liquid-filled. Except for the professional model *"Brunton Pocket Transit,"* induction damping has all but disappeared from the compass scene.

Sights

Some compasses come equipped with sights, which may or may not be a good thing. *Optical* (lensatic and prismatic) sights are most accurate and, in compasses of good quality, give results comparable to expensive surveying instruments.

When you look through an optical sight, you see image, graduated dial and a vertical intersect line, all in the same plane. The result — in a well built compass — is accuracy to a fraction of a degree.

Lensatic sights, like those on the old military field compass, are good or bad, depending on the precision of the sight assembly. The original American army lensatics could be read to two degrees of perfection or better. But the 10 dollar foreign copies which currently flood the market, are another matter. Most won't read within five degrees of a transit!

Combination mirror-vee sight: There's a pop-up mirror with a vertical line scribed through its center. You adjust the mirror to a 60 degree angle (so you can see the alignment of the needle in the capsule), turn your body (not the compass) until the needle is centered within a printed arrow on the dial, then peer across the gunsight vee on the cover top towards your objective. Sounds accurate, and it can be, if you're extremely meticulous. Fact is, you can do as well — often better — by simply holding the instrument waist high and looking straight ahead. Accuracy of the system depends in large measure on precision mounting of the mirror and your ability to keep everything in alignment while holding it all rock steady.

The problem with *all* non-optical sights is their very short sighting plane — akin to shooting accurately with a 2-inch barreled pistol. As explained, the accuracy of any sight depends on the precision and ruggedness of the mounting system. Unfortunately, most hinged compass sights lack the durability for long term precise alignment. For this reason, your best bet is to use the *"waist-high"* method of sighting which is explained at the end of this chapter.

Here's what you can expect from the various compass styles:

COMPASS TYPE	PROBABLE MAXIMUM ERROR WITHOUT PRACTICE	PROBABLE MAXIMUM ERROR WITH CONSIDERABLE PRACTICE	APPROXIMATE TIME TO TAKE AN ACCURATE BEARING
Optical sighting	1 degree	1/2 degree or less	15 seconds
Orienteering	4 degrees	1-1/2 degrees	10 seconds
Induction-damped cruiser	4 degrees	1-1/2 degrees	20 seconds
liquid-damped fixed-dial	10 degrees	5 degrees	15 seconds

Figure 3-4   Characteristics of various compass styles.

Declination

Some compasses have a mechanical adjustment for magnetic declination. This feature is quite inexpensive and is necessary only if you live in an area where declination values are large ... or if you are confused by the mathematics of its computation. See the next chapter for details.

Inclination

The earth behaves like a giant magnet and the closer you get to the poles, the greater the magnetic force. This causes the north end of the needle to dip down in the northern hemisphere and to rise in the southern hemisphere. Consequently, the compass needle must be balanced for the zone of operation so the needle will spin freely on its pivot.

Professional surveying instruments have a movable counter-weight on the needle tail, which can be re-positioned if necessary. Field compasses, however, come from the factory balanced for the zone of use. Most any compass you buy in the U.S. will work fine in North America. Hiking in Equador is another matter! Instruments which are balanced for far northern and southern zones are available on special order from the best compass makers.

Dial Graduations

The best compasses have dials which are graduated in one or two degree increments. More graduations than this simply clutters the dial. However, a lot of fine instruments have five degree graduations (especially those with small dials) and this is quite suitable for a field compass.

The rule is that you can interpolate a bearing by twice splitting the distance between the graduations on either side of the index. Thus, a two degree dial can be guestimated to one-half a degree; a five degree dial to one and one-fourth degrees, etc. So if you need the most precise readings, opt for finer graduations.

It's important to realize that precision bearings are only useful when combined with optical sighting systems. They are of little value in an Orienteering compass. That's because Orienteering instruments are almost never *"read."* Instead, the needle is aligned in the *"doghouse"* (printed arrow inside the capsule) and the direction-of-travel arrow on the base plate is followed. There is no need to read specific numbers. Indeed, Orienteering compasses need not be graduated at all!

How Much Does A Good Compass Cost?

At this writing, 20 bucks will buy all the compass you need for wilderness travel. Paying more won't necessarily buy more accuracy or versatility. Extra cost options like declination adjustments, night sights and sighting devices, drive up costs and add little utility. Fact is, the least expensive Orienteering models are suitable for the most complex lake and land navigation you're likely to encounter. You *don't* need a professional compass for touring the backcountry.

How To Use The *"Waist-High"* Method of Sighting Your Orienteering Compass

Here's the most accurate way to take a bearing to a distant object with an Orienteering compass:

Cradle the compass in your right hand and frame the dial with the thumb and forefinger of your left hand (Figure 3- 5). Forearms should be held gently but firmly against the body to provide a three point (triangular) position, the apex of which is the compass.

Figure 3-5
1) Cradle the compass in your right hand and frame
the dial with the thumb and forefinger of your left
hand. Be sure the "direction of travel" arrow on the
compass base plate is pointing *toward* your objective.

READ COMPASS AT INDEX
INSCRIBED ON DIAL

OBJECTIVE

Direction of travel

2) Turn the dial (housing) until the
north end of the magnetic needle
points to "N" on the dial (needle
framed inside orienting arrow in the
clear plastic capsule).

3) Read your bearing at the "index"
on the dial.

Locate the compass *directly* along the mid-line of your body,
just above your waist and a comfortable distance (about 6 inches)
away from your stomach.

Next, turn *your body* (not the compass) until the direction-of-
travel arrow on the compass base plate is pointing towards the
objective whose bearing you want to determine. Then, while holding
the base plate steady, turn the compass housing until the magnetic
needle is framed inside the orienting arrow *("doghouse")* in the
clear plastic capsule.

Now, take *three* "eye-shift" readings to your objective; that is, sight three times from the compass housing to the objective, *without* moving your head. When the alignment of everything — needle in doghouse, direction-of-travel arrow and objective — is perfect, read your bearing. It should be within two degrees of an optical transit.

How To Take An Accurate Bearing With A Fixed-Dial Compass

Although experienced wilderness travelers rely entirely on Orienteering style compasses, they frequently carry a small *"gum-ball machine"* compass as an emergency backup. Even a simple *"zipper pull"* compass can provide accurate directions if you know how to use it. Here's the recommended procedure:

1. Squarely face the objective whose bearing you wish to determine, then frame the compass between your thumbs and forefingers, as illustrated in Figure 3-6. Your index fingers form a triangle, the apex of which *"points"* to the objective.

Figure 3-6   A fixed dial compass can be used to take a reasonably accurate bearing if you use this procedure.

2, Now, rotate the compass between your fingers until the north end of the magnetic needle points to north on the dial.

3. Hold everything rock steady and read your bearing at the point where your forefingers touch. You should be within five degrees of a transit.

Now that you've mastered the workings of map and compass, you're ready to use them together as a complete navigational system. The next chapter shows you how.

4. NAVIGATION BASICS

First, Some Compass Basics

The compass is graduated in degrees. There are 360 degrees in the compass circle, or *"rose"* (Figure 4-1). The cardinal directions (north, south, east, and west) are each 90 degrees apart. *Memorize* the eight principal points of the compass, and their relationship to the map. This will help eliminate the most common of compass errors — the 180 degree error.

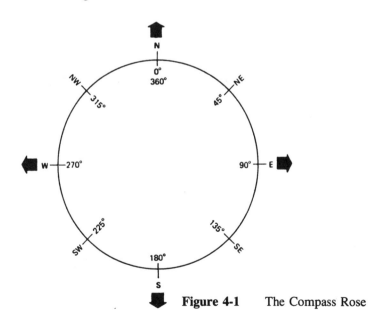

Figure 4-1   The Compass Rose

For example: Assume you are fishing *"Lost Lake"* (Figure 4-2) and are anchored at the peninsula at Point E. You want to go to *"Mud Island,"* which lies 1-1/2 miles to the east. With your orienteering compass, you inadvertently compute a bearing of 270 degrees, which is 180 degrees in error. However, if you had mentally superimposed the compass rose over point E, *before* you determined the map bearing to the island, you'd have instantly discovered your mistake.

It is not uncommon to transfer data from map to compass and make serious directional mistakes. *A knowledge of your approximate direction of travel should be known before you get down to specifics!*

Using The Compass To Determine A Map Bearing

A *bearing* is one of the 360 degree directions of the compass rose. It is always measured *clockwise* from north (either true, grid or magnetic) to the place you want to go (your objective). For now, we'll forget about the differences between the *"three norths"* and simply reference our bearing to *"true north,"* which is at the top of the Lost Lake map in Figure 4-2.

Assume you plan to fish the south end of Long Island, on Lost Lake. That's where the big ones are, or so you've heard! Getting to Long Island from your location at A, should be easy; just head north up the east shoreline, counting bays as you go. When you see Mud Island, hang a left around the north edge and you'll run right into your treasure spot. Easy as pie.

Don't you believe it! Look at the map scale. It's more than 12 miles to Long Island. Even on a clear day, it's doubtful you'll be able to see the intermediate islands or bays along the way. Islands and shoreline will blend to oneness. Because of wind and waves you'll lose all sense of distance traveled. You can easily mistake one of the closer islands for Mud Island, or you can get turned around completely and become convinced that a channel between islands is a large bay, or vice versa.

But getting to Long Island is easy, if you have a systematic plan and a compass. The important thing, is to keep track of where you are *all the time* — easy enough if you compute bearings to

Figure 4-2

Lost Lake Practice Map

Average Magnetic
Declination Equals
6 East.

LOST LAKE

intermediate check points along the way and reaffirm your position at each point. Here the procedure:

First, arbitrarily pick a check point on the map. It should be some place that's reasonably close and easily identifiable — a small island, the tip of a peninsula, a prominent bay, etc. You may or may not be able to see these check points (or *"attack points,"* as they're called in orienteering terms) from your location at A.

You decide that your first attack point will be the southern tip of Horseshoe Island, 2-3/4 miles away. Begin by guestimating the bearing from your location at A to your objective at B. You'll be heading *northwest*, or about 315 degrees. *Remember* that number!

Next, determine the actual compass bearing from A to B, with your orienteering compass (preferred) or a protractor.

Protractor Method

(Use this if you *don't* have an orienteering compass)
1. Draw a line from A to B.
2. Center your protractor over A and align *"protractor north"* with *"true north"* on your map (Figure 4-3). Remember, *"true north"* is at the *top* of your map. Its direction is indicated by the starred leg of the declination diagram (more on this later) in the right map margin.
3. Read the protractor at the line intersect. You get 290 degrees.
4. Compare this figure (290°) with your guestimate of 315°. Are the two within 90° of one another? Good. You haven't made an error: You *know* you're going in the right direction!

Computing the Bearing With An Orienteering Compass

1. Place either the left or right edge of the compass base plate over point A. Place the forward edge of the *same side* of the

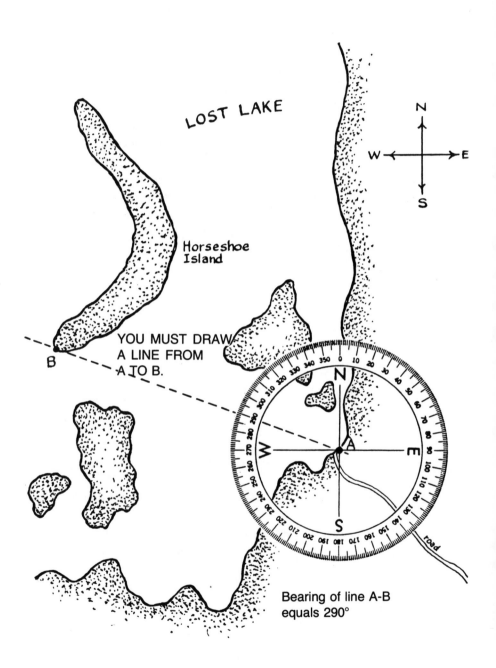

Figure 4-3   Using a protractor to determine a map bearing.

Figure 4-4   **Orienteering compass on map — showing how to align it.**

base plate on point B. Your compass is now pointing in the direction you want to go — *from A to B*, not from B to A (Figure 4-4).

2. While *holding the base plate tightly in position*, turn the compass housing until north on the dial points to the top (true north) of the map. *Caution:* Don't use the magnetic needle! Your direction of travel — 290 degrees — is now locked onto the dial and can be read at the index inscribed on the compass base.

3. Now ... while holding the compass in front of you with the direction-of-travel arrow inscribed on the base pointing *away* from your body, rotate your body with the compass until the magne-

tic needle points to north on the dial. Look straight ahead. You are now facing 290 degrees — towards Horseshoe Island.

4.   All that's necessary now is to locate a notch or visible incongruity on the horizon that you can identify as being on this course of travel. Put your compass away, fire up your motor and cruise on towards your objective.

Note: This is identical to the *"waist-high"* sighting method, described on page 34, except that instead of shooting a bearing to a distant point, you're computing it from a map.

Okay, test time. Use your Orienteering compass or protractor to compute the *"true"* bearings from points A through G on the Lost Lake map. Check your answers below. Don't try to compute *"distance," "travel time,"* or *"magnetic bearing."* We'll get to these later.

ANSWERS TO LOST LAKE EXERCISE

Point	True Bearing	Distance (miles)	Approximate Travel Time	Magnetic Bearing (to be set on your compass)
A to B	290°	2¾	1½ hours	284°
B to C	341°	1½	¾ hour	335°
C to D	15°	4/5	20 minutes	9°
D to E	338°	4	2 hours	332°
E to F	274°	3¼	1½ hours	268°
F to G	244°	1⅛	½ hour	238°
G to H	227°	2½	1¼ - 1½ hours	221°

H to portage (paddle north up the shoreline to portage): Time -- about 15 minutes.

Aiming Off

Proceeding from attack point to attack point is as useful on land as it is on water, with one exception: Trees! Getting around them necessarily means re-establishing your bearing after every *"run in"* — not impossible, but awkward enough to preclude pinpoint targeting of your objective. For this reason, precise compass bearings are usually modified by *"aiming off."* This simple procedure ensures you'll hit your objective, head-on. Consider the following scenario:

You've parked your car at point A in Figure 4-5 and have hiked the trail to McClaren Lake (point B). You may take any one of the three routes on the return leg: 1) Hike the trail back to A — a weaving, time-consuming route, though one on which you can't possibly get confused. 2) Follow the trail to its end at Goldbar Lake (C), then continue on down the creek to the road at D. From here, walk one and one-half miles east to your car.

But wait! Look at the topography between C and D. The value of each contour line, in feet, is labeled and circled on the map, and the *contour interval*, as given in the map legend, is 50 feet. Arrows mark where each contour crosses the creek. As you can see, the creek drops 300 feet (1000 minus 700) in the mile and a half distance from Goldbar Lake to the road, and likely, it's all through a tangle of head high brush. Working your way down this steep slope, climbing over downed trees and tag alder, might take much longer — and be far more unpleasant — than backtracking over the trail.

However, there's another alternative — a straight compass shot from B to A. You'll be going overland so it'll be tough sledding. And you'll have to avoid the scattered ponds and wade a few creeks. But it will spell ADVENTURE — the reason why you came here in the first place. And, it would be awesomely remote. If you used your compass, you can't get lost.

Let's do it! Here's the procedure.

If you compute a direct bearing from your present location at B, to A, your chance of arriving on target at the road junction is very small. After all, you'll be climbing up and down hills, skirting ponds and brush piles. That you won't be able to maintain a precise course over this rough ground is a forgone fact. Better to compensate for this known error by *"aiming off"* a bit to the west — say to point E. Granted, you'll probably miss E, but you *will* strike the road somewhere east or west of it. Once you hit the road just follow it *east* to your starting point. Simple, isn't it?

If *aiming off"* is useful on land, it's even more useful on water. For example: Suppose you're located at point G on the Lost Lake map (Figure 4-2). You want to take the portage trail that leads to the South Arm of Maze Lake, just north of H. There are three

Figure 4-5 Aiming off map.

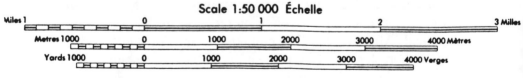

Scale 1:50 000 Échelle

Declination = 10° East   Contour Interval = 50 feet

portages leading our of Bay 3, but only ones goes to South Arm. From G to the South Arm trail is about three miles. A 4-degree error over this distance would cause you to miss your objective by at least 1100 feet (remember, one degree of compass error equals 92 feet per mile of ground error), or nearly one- fourth of a mile — enough to send you scurrying down the wrong trail.

The solution is to *"aim off"* to *"H"* — an unidentifiable point just south of the trail. Then, when you reach the shoreline, turn right (north.) The first path you come to is the right one.

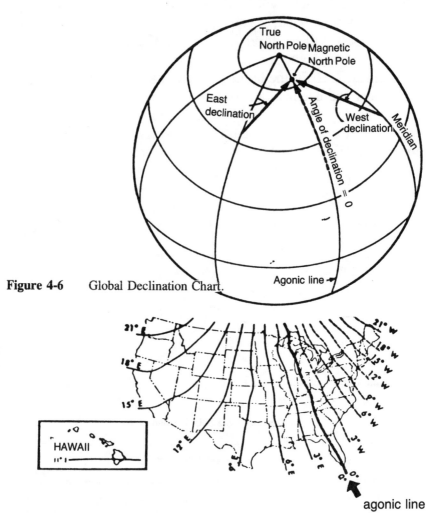

Figure 4-6   Global Declination Chart.

Figure 4-7   Standard Declination Chart:

Declination

A compass points (actually, it doesn't point — it lines up with the earth's magnetic field) to *magnetic* north, not *true* north. This angular difference, called *declination* must be considered whenever you use your compass (Figures 4-6, 4-7). In the eastern United

States the declination is westerly; in the western United States it's easterly. If you live right on the imaginary line which goes directly through both the true and magnetic north poles (called the *agonic*) line, your declination will be zero.

On the other hand, if you live east or west of the agonic line, your compass will be in error, since the true north pole is not in the same place as the magnetic north pole. As you can see from the declination chart, the farther away you are from the agonic line, the greater the declination. Moreover, the magnetic pole is constantly moving; because of this, declination will vary from year to year as well as place to place. Consequently, it's not possible for compass makers to factory-adjust a compass to account for this variation.

To find the exact declination for your area, consult your topographic map. You'll find the declination value in a diagram in the lower map margin. It will look something like this:

Figure 4-8
Declination Value Diagram.

Use diagram only to obtain numerical values
APPROXIMATE MEAN DECLINATION 1962
FOR CENTER MAP
Annual change decreasing 6.3'

Note that the *"legs"* of the declination diagram in Figure 4-8 *are not* drawn to angular scale (some diagrams *are*). The angles are slightly exaggerated for clarity — a note to that effect appears in the legend. Consequently, you shouldn't use the direction of the magnetic flag as an accurate pointing for your compass. Instead, adjust the instrument mathematically, as explained in the following section.

1.   The star (★) indicates the direction of true north. This leg of the diagram runs parallel to a line of longitude.

2.   The flag (/) points to magnetic north. If the flag is to the right (east) of the true north star, the area declination is east. If it's to the left of the star, the declination is west.

3.   The black sphere (●) indicates the direction of the grid lines on the map. *Remember* topographic maps do not have lines of longitude imprinted on their faces, but they do have grid lines. The two *are not* the same! When you peel the skin off a globe (earth) and lay it flat, you distort the curved meridians. This distortion — or variation from true north, is reported in all declination diagrams.

Interpreting the Diagram

In Figure 4-8, grid north is thirteen minutes *west* of true north. Disregard the 4 mil number. That's for military use.*

Magnetic north is 31°24' (31°37'- 0°13') east of true north (you should round it off to 31 degrees.) This is the direction your compass needle will point. It is also the value of the *declination*, which is defined as *the angle between true north and magnetic north*.

You can also determine *grid declination* from the diagram. It is the angle between *grid north* and magnetic north — in this case, 31°37' east, or *32 degrees*, when round off. The section on grid declination on page 49 tells you how to use this important figure.

Dealing With Declination

Check out the declination on the Lost Lake map. It equals 6 degrees east. There are no grid lines on this map, hence, no need to identify *"grid"* north.

As stated, maps are almost always drawn in their true perspective (any variation here is so small it can be ignored). So any bearing you determine *from the map* by using the top of the map or the east or west border (line of longitude) as a *"north"* reference, is, by definition, a *true* bearing. The bearings you computed in the A through G "point to point," exercise were therefore all *true* bearings. *Now, you must change these true values to magnetic ones which will be set on your compass* and followed on the ground — easy enough, if you remember the simple rhyme:

Declination east — compass least (subtract east declination from your map direction).

---

*The military compass is graduated in "mils." There are 6400 mils in a circle. North is zero mils, east is 1600 mils, south is 3200 mils, etc. Mils are further subdivided into tenths and hundredths. Minutes and seconds are not used.

Declination west — compass best (add west declination to your map direction).

Your true bearing from A to B in the Lost Lake exercise was 290 degrees. Change it to a magnetic bearing by application of the rhyme. *Subtract* six degrees and you get 284. Adjust your compass for this new heading and take off. You'll hit point B head-on.

Conversely, if the declination were west, you would *add* its value (290 + 6 = 296) to your compass reading.

Note: It makes no difference in which direction (north, south, east or west, or something in-between) you are going on the map sheet. If declination is *east*, you *always* subtract its value from your true map bearing. If it's west , you add it. If this is confusing, you may want to buy a compass which can be adjusted for declination.

Okay, test time ... again. Convert all your *true* Lost Lake bearings to magnetic ones. Answers are on page 43.

Grid Declination

Grid lines take the guess work out of aligning your protractor or orienteering compass to map north. Remember, however, that *grid lines don't point true north*, so you'll have to compensate for their variation.

Any bearing you compute off a map, using *grid north* (any grid line) as the north reference line is, by definition, a *grid bearing*. Before you can follow this bearing on the ground, you must first convert it to a *magnetic bearing* by application of the *"east is least/west is best"* rhyme.

The grid declination in Figure 4-8, is 31°37' east, or 32°, when rounded off. Subtract 32° from your grid bearing and set this value on your compass. That's all there is to it. The procedure is identical to that used to change a true bearing to a magnetic one.

In truth, we're splitting hairs here, for grid north is so close to true north (just 13 minutes away) that the difference is meaningless. However, this isn't always the case, so check out the values before you commit to your *"accurate"* field bearings. Admittedly, true and grid north seldom vary by much more than three degrees, so for typical field use, the two can usually be considered as one.

Tape Method Of Adjusting
The Compass For Declination

If you don't want to mess with the mechanics of adding or subtracting declination values from your true or grid bearings, you can *"adjust"* your compass to compensate. Here's how.

Given: You have computed a *true* map bearing of 60 degrees to your objective. The area declination, is 10 degrees east.

Procedure: Place a narrow piece of tape across the face of the compass housing so that it goes over the needle pivot and intersects both the 10 degree and 190 degree marks. Your compass is now adjusted to compensate for a 10 degree east declination.

Now ... hold the compass in front of you and find the bearing on the ground — only *don't* frame the magnetic needle in the *"doghouse"* (printed arrow in the capsule) as is customary. Instead, align it with the tape mark, which is 10 degrees east of north. Note that you are actually facing a bearing of 50 (60-10) degrees.

Conversely, if the declination were 10 degrees *west*, you would apply the tape so that it intersected the 350 degree (that's 10°west) and 170 degree marks. As you might guess, the mechanical declination adjustments on sophisticated compasses use this very procedure.

Adjusting Your Map For Declination

You can also adjust your map for declination by drawing lines, which run parallel to the north magnetic pole, across its face. Then, when you compute map headings, just align the printed arrow in the capsule of your orienteering compass with these lines, rather than *"map north"* (top of the map). All competitive orienteering maps are set up like this. However, the system works much better with small orienteering maps than with 2-1/2 foot square topos. Try drawing parallel lines across a standard sized topographic map and you'll see why. Best stick with a more conventional treatment of declination.

Updating The Declination

The magnetic poles are constantly moving. Their location changes from year to year (and minute to minute). Movements are subtle, however — generally small enough that only surveyors interested in extreme accuracy need worry about them.

The problem only surfaces when you're working off a very old map. For example, the legend in Figure 4-8 states ... APPROX-IMATE MEAN DECLINATION 1962 ... annual change decreasing 6.3'.

This means that magnetic north (the flag) is moving *westward* (decreasing) by 6.3 minutes per year. Updating the declination to 1989 is easy:

1.   Determine the elapsed years (1989-1962 = 27 years).

2.   Multiply the annual change by the elapsed years (6.3' x 27 years) = 170.1 minutes.

3.   Convert minutes to whole degrees (170.1/60 = 2.8 or ... *3 degrees*.

4.   Subtract this figure from the 1962 declination of 31 degrees (31°-3°=28°). Your declination for 1989 is 28° east.

Note: to update the *Grid declination*, merely subtract three degrees from the grid-magnetic angle of 32°. Answer: 29° east.

Position By Triangulation

Suppose you're lost on a large, mazelike lake, but you can recognize two or more topographical features off in the distance. Use your orienteering compass (or protractor and conventional compass) to find your position by *"triangulation."*

Figure 4-9   Position of Triangulation:

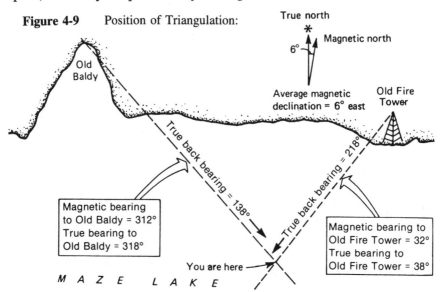

Pick out one point on the horizon which you can identify —
Old Baldy, in this case (see Figure 4-9). Shoot a magnetic bearing
to the point (bearing = 312 degrees). Change this magnetic bearing
to a *true* bearing by *reverse* application of the rhyme: 312° + 6°
= 318°. Draw the back (reciprocal) bearing (318°- 180° = 138°)
through Old Baldy, using your compass base plate and a sharp
pencil.

Tip: When using an orienteering compass you don't have to
compute the back bearing at all. Simply set 318° on the compass
dial, place your pencil point on Old Baldy, and put the forward
edge of one side of the base plate against the pencil point. Rotate
the entire compass in an arc about the pencil until north on the dial
(not the needle) points to the top (true north) of the map. Caution:
Do not turn the compass housing during this operation, since the
true bearing which you just computed to Old Baldy (318°) is set
on the dial. This procedure will not work if you change the dial
setting!

Now ... using the base plate as a straight edge, draw your
line. Repeat the exercise using another point which you can identify
(the old fire tower). You are located where the two lines cross.

Okay, time now for another test, using the Lost Lake map.
You can identify Dunker Hill at a magnetic bearing of 253 degrees
and Kaby Lookout at a magnetic bearing of 4 degrees. Where are
you located? Clue: Don't forget to apply the declination. You'll
find the answer on page 54.

Relocating A Good Fishing Spot
By Triangulation

You don't need to identify points on a map to use triangulation.
In fact, you don't need a map at all! Suppose you've discovered a
real hot spot — the fish are biting like crazy. You definitely want
to come here again! Problem is, there are no identifying landmarks
to guide the way. And the fishing hole is small, just a dozen yards
in diameter. How on earth will you find this place again?

Easy! Just shoot compass bearings to two or more places on
the shoreline. The tall pine on the right (Figure 4-10) and broken
down cabin at left, are ideal. But your points need not be so sophisticated. A moss-covered boulder or leaning tree will do. Anything

Figure 4-10   Relocating a good fishing spot by triangulation.

that won't *"run off"* will work. Since you don't have a map, there's
no need to compute back bearings, or to draw intersecting lines.
Instead, simply record the numbers in a notebook for future reference. Next time you come here, look for the cabin and cliff. Then,
position yourself where the two bearings match.

Free Triangulation

This is the same as *"two point triangulation,"* except you need
just one reference line. Assume you're hiking along the railroad
track in Figure 4-11 and want to establish your exact position. In
the distance you see a large hill which stands out boldly among the
flatlands. You shoot a compass bearing to the hill and get 156
degrees.

Declination = 10°East

Figure 4-11   Free triangulation diagram

Convert this *magnetic* reading to a *true* direction by reverse application of the *"rhyme."* 156° + 10° = 166°. Next, determine the *back bearing* (166° + 180° = 346°) and plot it on the map. You're located where the line crosses the track.

Use free triangulation any place you can establish a single line of reference — a road, trail, river, creek, lakeshore or powerline.

ANSWER TO TRIANGULATION PROBLEM
You are located at the north end of Horseshoe Island.

5. TRICKS OF THE TRADE

If you've progressed this far, you're just short of being expert with map and compass. You can now compute map bearings, convert them to magnetic readings, and chart a course through tangled brush or the maze of islands on a fog bound lake. You know all about aiming off, triangulation and declination, plus a wealth of other navigation procedures.

So congratulations on your hard-earned confidence. You're *"almost"* ready to cope with the worst of times on the best of terms. What you need now is practice, practice, practice ... plus a working knowledge of some tricks of the trade. Here are a few:

Navigation At Night

Over the years I've done a fair amount of black night canoe travel on large sprawling lakes. Most memorable was the time I camped in the Boundary Waters Canoe Area of Minnesota and was awakened to find three bears merrily munching dehydrated prunes which my teen group had carelessly thrown about. We blew whistles, clanged pans and yelled loudly. No luck. The bruins remained oblivious to the racket and kept right on eating.

When they knocked down one tent, we decided it was time to leave. Within minutes we struck camp and put to sea. There was no moon or stars; just full cloud cover and vast nothingness. Visibility was a flat zero.

Fortunately, I had a flashlight and my Silva Ranger compass. I carefully plotted a bee line for a distant island which had a campsite. Then I set the compass on the floor of my canoe and unerringly kept the luminous point on the magnetic needle aligned with the glowing *"aid dots"* which flanked it.

Before we dipped paddles, I carefully computed the distance from our location to the island. It was almost exactly three miles. At an approximate paddling speed of two cautious miles per hour, we should arrive on target in 90 minutes. I set my watch alarm and peeled out into the blackness of the night.

Exactly eighty minutes later, we touched shore. There was the island ... and the welcome campsite.

Moral: You need more than good bearings for black night travel. You also need to keep accurate track of your distance and time!

Problem: Calculate the distance between points on the Lost Lake practice map in Chapter Four. Assume a travel speed of two miles per hour. Check your answers on page 43.

Traveling overland on a dead dark night, is another matter. Some years ago, as a forester with the Bureau of Land Management in Oregon, I was lost for three days in the mountains, south of Coos Bay. Again, I had my trusty Silva, but this time, no map. Referencing was a *"matter of the mind:"* I knew highway 101 was about 60 miles due west. I tried to travel the first night, but it was no use. After a number of life-threatening falls, I gave up in disgust and waited till sunrise.

Around noon of the third day, I struck a logging road and the sound of a clanging diesel tractor. Humility? You bet. When I returned to work the next day, I never told a soul. After all ... foresters *"don't get lost!"*

Outdoor books are rich with tales of men who traveled the haunting wilds with only the stars or a simple compass to guide them. Of course, it *can* be done and has been done, but the risks of injury are very real.

However, night travel takes on new dimensions if the sky is gentle gray, or you have a full moon or a powerful headlamp to guide the way. And oh yes, don't rely on luminous compass points to keep on track. Compass *"night sights"* are very primitive: Without frequent light to recharge their chemical *"batteries,"* they fail. None will last the night. A flashlight — or other light source — is essential.

As to navigation by the stars (discounting *celestial* navigation, of course), I know of no one who has ever had to resort to such folly. If you are lost or without a compass, you have no business traveling at night, and if you do have a compass you certainly don't need the stars. Moreover, trees and topographical features sometimes prevent you from keeping the North Star in view. Such star navigation makes interesting reading, but it's impractical. However, if you're interested in this sort of thing, check out a Boy Scout Handbook or standard text on surveying.

River Navigation

Everything in this book has been necessarily centered around land and lake navigation. After all, that's where you'll be navigating most of the time. But suppose you want to canoe or raft a wild, brawny river. Are there navigational concerns other than those mentioned in Chapter Two?

You bet! With the impact of man on river systems, it is becoming more and more important for river users to know what the water conditions are before they go afloat. Many local and even far northern rivers are now dam controlled, and are very dangerous at high water or impossible during the *"walking levels"* of late summer. Barbed wire fences strung across rivers maim and kill boaters each year, and the people who string these fences usually have the law on their side. Each year, we read about canoeists and fishermen who inadvertently paddled over a dam because they didn't know it was there.

If you boat rivers, you must be able to accurately locate and identify dams, rapids, fences and other obstacles which can endanger your trip. The symbols for many of these appear on your topographic map. But not all. And frequently, what's there is incorrect. Here are some ways to out-fox the inadequacies of your map.

1.   Continually check the *level* of the tree line as you paddle along. If tree heights fall off suddenly, there's a dam or falls ahead.

2.   Maps do not indicate obstacles which are the result of river turbulence. Waves pile up on the *outside* of bends, and so does debris. Except in very low water, you should always stay on the *inside* curves of a river.

3.   It is very difficult to fix your position on a river. A compass will be useful for rough directions only. Of course, you can reaffirm your location at major bends, rapids, or incoming streams. Or, you may be fortunate enough to locate an identifiable object upon which you can plot a line of free triangulation.

Lastly, some of the best maps of river conditions are the people who live in the area. Always check with them before embarking on a river, even if you've run it many times. Be aware, however that locals tend to exaggerate the dangers of their river. So especially seek out foresters or professional people who work in the area. Outdoors people will generally tell it like it is ... or at least they'll exaggerate less.

And if one day your dreams take you to the far north where rivers run cold and help is an airplane ride away, you'll need to know (ABSOLUTELY KNOW!) your precise location at all times. Contrary to what you may have read or heard, compasses are generally quite reliable near the arctic circle — that is, if you can correctly apply the declination — which may change with each few miles you travel!

Navigating Streams And Moose Trails

Finding your way through a maze of beaver streams and moose trails call for resourcefulness. Remember, modern maps are made from aerial photos, and if you can't see the sky because of a dense tree canopy or tall grass, the plane-mounted camera can't see the stream. Therefore, your map may be in error in these places, though the general flow of the water course — minus the switchbacks — is usually accurate.

The heads and mouths of small streams are almost always plotted correctly, but deciphering the maze in between often calls for a ready compass. Moreover, stream beds are constantly changing and these changes will not be reflected on a topographic map that is many years old.

Some hints for navigating small meandering streams; 1) Where a stream forks, take the route with the strongest flow, even if it looks more restrictive than a broader channel. If there is no discernible current, note which way the grass bends in the channel and follow. 2) Check your compass frequently; don't rely on your map, especially if it is many years old. 3) If you come to a dead end and see a portage trail, scout it before you carry your canoe or boat across. Your *"portage"* may simply be a heavily used animal trail which leads to a connecting tributary or dead-end pond.

Your Watch As A Compass

Although of questionable accuracy, direction finding using a watch is at times convenient when you want a rough, quick direction but you don't want to get out your compass. If your watch is correctly set for the time zone in which you're traveling, just hold the watch horizontal and point the hour hand at the sun. Half way between the hour hand and twelve o'clock is south. Such showmanship will impress your friends when things get dull on a long trip (though Robert Owendorff pointed out the unreliability of this method in *"How to Get Lost in One Simple Lesson,"* in the January, 1973 issue of the Isaak Walton League magazine).

By the way, you can also use your compass as a watch. Just keep in mind the hourly positions of the sun, which are ...

6 A.M. — east
9 A.M. southeast
12 noon — south
3 P.M. southwest
6 P.M. west

Baselines

Most every book on wilderness navigation has a chapter devoted to *"the lost hunter"* — re-locating your remote camp, finding the remains of the deer you shot, etc. But it's all simply a matter of *"baselines;"* that is, you establish a reliable handrail (road, stream, powerline, etc.) then use it as a reference line for your bearings. Figure 1-2 is a typical example of this relationship — one which again proves the importance of a map. Note, however, that you don't need a formal map to travel the backwoods with confidence. A mind relationship is often enough. My three day *"confusion"* in the Oregon woods, is a case in point. I *knew* highway 101 was due west. And that was sufficient!

As you can see, there's no substitute for common sense. To this add a good map and compass and a practiced hand, and you'll have all the tools you need to confidently navigate the backcountry.

APPENDIX 1

GOOD FIELD COMPASSES

There are dozens of good orienteering compasses. Here are some with which I've had personal experience, and can highly recommend.

Price Guidelines
A — Under ten dollars, at this writing.
B — Ten to twenty dollars.
C — Twenty to forty dollars.
D — Over forty dollars.

Silva Ranger

Top of the Silva line, this has been the favored compass of professional foresters for years and it serves as the official military compass in many countries. Has a mirror sight, declination adjustment, rubber feet to prevent slippage on maps, clinometer for slope determination and graduated map scales on the plastic base plate. This is my personal choice for a *"serious"* field compass. Price: C

Silva *Huntsman*

Smallest of the orienteering compasses. It's about the size of a penny match book, yet is nearly as accurate as full size models. You can pin it on your shirt when hunting or carry it comfortably in a breast pocket. Expect two degree accuracy and famed Silva reliability. The Huntsman is my favorite *"every day"* field compass. No sights or declination features. Price: B

Silva *Landmark*, Type 27

Identical to the *"Huntsman"* but features a cover and mirror-sight. Less compact but more rugged. Price: B

Silva *Explorer*, Type 3

A compact full size orienteering compass that has luminous points, magnifying glass, map scales and a non-mechanical declination feature. Best buy in the Silva line. Price: B

Brunton *9020*

No bells or whistles on this one; just a simple base plate with map scales and a revolving capsule with built-in declination adjustment. All edges are rounded so it carries comfortably in a shirt pocket. Price: A

Suunto *MC-1D Professional*

Nearly identical to the venerable Silva Ranger, except for no rubber feet and different map scales. The MC-1D shares top honors with the Ranger as *the* compass you ought to carry when the chips are down. Price: C

Suunto *M-3D Leader*

Take the Suunto MC-1D and eliminate the clinometer, cover and mirror and you have the M-3D. The compass has a ratchet adjusted declination device, rubber feet, magnifying glass and map scales. Also, circle and triangle templates for competitive orienteering. This compass will do anything the MC-1D will do, yet it costs half the price. Best buy in the Suunto line. Price: B

Silva *T-24 Wrist Compass*

A watch sized modified orienteering compass that's designed to be worn on the wrist. The T-24 makes a great boat compass (strap it around a seat brace or thwart) and is great for spelunking. However, it is not versatile enough to take the place of a full frame orienteering compass. Price: B

Suunto *KB-14*

The KB-14 is an *optical sighting* compass. It has no built-in protractor, map scales, magnifier or other niceties. It is however, the most accurate hand compass you'll find, with accuracy to better than 15 minutes of arc. This is *the* compass for professional work or whenever exact bearings are required. Price: D

Addresses

Silva Divison	Suunto Division	Brunton/Lakota
Johnson Camping, Inc.	Optimus, Inc.	620 E. Monroe Ave.
P.O. Box 966	P.O. Box 1950	Riverton, WY 82501
Binghamton, NY 13902	Bridgeport, CT 06601	

APPENDIX 2

COMMON U.S. MAP SYMBOLS

TOPOGRAPHIC MAP SYMBOLS			
Primary highway	▬▬▬	Gravel beach or glacial moraine	
Secondary highway	▬▭▬	Woods (green)	
Light duty road	═══	Scrub (green)	
Unimproved road	=====	Orchard (green)	
Trail	-------	Rock bare or awash	✳
Bridge		Group of rocks bare or awash	✳ ✳ ✳
Building: small; large	■ ▨	Sunken rock	+
Cemetery: small; large	⊺ Cem	Intermittent stream	
Standard gauge single track; station	+—+—■+	Disappearing stream	
Abandoned track	-+-+-	Large falls; large rapids	
Power Transmission line; pole; tower		Masonary dam	
Telephone or telegraph line	-----	Intermittent lake or pond	
Quarry or open pit mine	✕	Dry lake	
Mine tunnel or cave entrance	≺	Water well; spring or seep	o ⸰
Sand or mud area, dunes or shifting sand		Marsh or swamp	

63

Appendix 3...
Common Terms

Agonic Line: A line of zero declination. At any point along this imaginary line, the compass will point true north.

Aiming Off: The navigator aims to the right or left of his objective, rather than straight at it. This creates a purposeful error in a known direction, which helps in targeting the objective. See page 43 for details.

Attack Point: A point on the map that is easy to identify on land (hill top, road junction, railroad crossing, etc). Same as a "check point".

Back Bearing: Also called reciprocal bearing. It is the opposite direction from which you came. Or, 180 degrees plus or minus your forward bearing.

Base line: A "hand-rail" that's used as a reference line for positioning when afield. The navigator works on one side or the other of the base line. A return bearing is plotted to the base line, which is then followed "home".

Base Plate: The ruled plastic base of an orienteering compass.

Bearing: A direction, in degrees, from where you are to where you want to go. Technically, it's a horizontal angle measured from north to your direction of travel.

Cardinal Points: The primary directions—north, east, south, west.

Compasses: See index for compass types and their differences.

Compass Rose: The 360 degrees of the compass circle.

Contour Interval: The difference in elevation (usually above sea level) from one contour line to another.

Contour Lines: Light brown lines on a map which indicate height above sea level.

Declination: The direction in which the compass needle points. More accurately, it's the angular difference between "true" north and magnetic north, or between grid north and magnetic north (called "grid declination"). Expressed in degrees east or west of the agonic line.

Declination Diagram: A diagram in the legend of topographic maps which gives the value of the area declination.

Doghouse: A slang term for the printed arrow inside the housing of orienteering compasses. When the "dog" is in the "house"(magnetic needle inside printed arrow of housing), the compass is properly oriented.

Direction-of-Travel Arrow: An arrow inscribed on the plastic base plate of orienteering compasses points towards your objective when the compass is properly oriented (needle centered in the "doghouse").

Grid Lines: Interconnecting lines superimposed over the face of topographic maps.

Grid North: The direction the grid lines point with respect to true north.

Handrail: A topographic feature which you can follow to your objective. Examples: Road, river, creek, power line, trail, or lakeshore.

Housing: The part of the compass which contains the magnetic needle.

Index: A master map which contains information for ordering topographical maps. Also, the place on a compass where the bearing is read.

Intercardinal Points: Intermediate compass points—northeast, southeast, southwest, northwest.

Latitude: The distance in degrees, north or south of the equator.

Longitude: The distance in degrees, east or west of the prime meridian located at Greenwich, England.

Magnetic North: The direction the compass needle points.

Map aid lines: Parallel lines inside the housing of orienteering compasses. When these are aligned to map north, the compass will give a proper bearing you can follow on the ground.

Meridians: Same as lines of longitude. Meridians run true north and south.

NCIC: (National Cartographic Information Service): the federal clearing house for special purpose maps and cartographic information.

North: There are three norths—true (geographic), magnetic (direction the compass needle points), and grid (direction the grid lines run).

Orienteering: A competitive sport which combines cross-country running and compass directions to locate specific points (called controls) on the ground.

Parallels: Lines of latitude. These run "parallel" to the equator.

Planimetric Map: A map that does not indicate elevation above sea level. Example, a common road map.

Protractor: A plastic arc used for measuring angles.

Scale: The relationship between map and ground distance. Expressed as a representative fraction such as, 1:250,000.

Symbols: Icons on maps which depict primarily man-made features.

Topographic Map: A map that shows topography in three dimensions with the aid of contour lines.

U.S.G.S. (United States Geological Survey): Place where you order topographic maps.

Variation: A nautical term for declination.

INDEX